AWAY WITH WORDS

Young Writers' 16th Annual Poetry Competition

It is feeling and force of imagination that make us eloquent.

How can I not dream while writing?
The blank page gives a right to dream.

Verses From Kent

Edited by Lynsey Hawkins

 Young**Writers**

First published in Great Britain in 2007 by:
Young Writers
Remus House
Coltsfoot Drive
Peterborough
PE2 9JX
Telephone: 01733 890066
Website: www.youngwriters.co.uk

SB ISBN 978-1 84602 808 3

Foreword

This year, the Young Writers' *Away With Words* competition proudly presents a showcase of the best poetic talent selected from thousands of up-and-coming writers nationwide.

Young Writers was established in 1991 to promote the reading and writing of poetry within schools and to the young of today. Our books nurture and inspire confidence in the ability of young writers and provide a snapshot of poems written in schools and at home by budding poets of the future.

The thought, effort, imagination and hard work put into each poem impressed us all and the task of selecting poems was a difficult but nevertheless enjoyable experience.

We hope you are as pleased as we are with the final selection and that you and your family continue to be entertained with *Away With Words Verses From Kent* for many years to come.

Contents

The Channel School

The Thomas Aveling School

The Poems

Homeless

Just fears and dread
Without a bed,
All alone and with no home,
No one around, just an empty sound,
As I feel cold with no blanket to hold,
I know the winter's coming on,
When the sun goes down for too long.

Becky Rhodes (14)
Hartsdown Technology College

Always . . . Never . . .

Always the shoulder to cry on
Never the person crying on the shoulder.

Always the one asking the questions,
Never the one answering them.

Always the one being laughed at
Never the one laughing.

Always the victim
Never the bully.

Always the most unimportant part
Never the most important.

Becky Tumber (15)
Hartsdown Technology College

The Sly Fox

Creeping around in the dark night
The sly fox is looking for something to bite,
Crawling around low on the ground,
Where in the world can his food be found?
Then in the background
The sly fox hears something bouncing around,
At last - he says this is what I found.

Steven Stembridge (15)
Hartsdown Technology College

My Mum

My mum's my best friend,
As kind as can be.
There is not enough she can do
For my brother Jack and me.
Cooking, cleaning, ironing,
She is always on the go,
Always cheerful and happy,
I never see her low.
Whenever we're in trouble
And don't know what to do
We can always turn to Mother
And she will pull us though.
She's kind, generous and loving
And there's one more thing I must say
That I love my mum more and more
Each and every day.
I love you Mum.

Chanelle Smethers (15)
Hartsdown Technology College

Despair

Blackness covered all I see and all I touch,
No feeling of pain just sorrow,
My hand keeps a loose grip of the sword I held
And I've turned to become a true shadow.

So many battles with those two blades,
My body unable to move, blood on my lips,
And I speak no words as I stare
At my own blade's reflection.

A white knight on white bloom horse
With its silver hair shiny around,
Walks into the sunken temple of the forgotten city,
Many wailing willows lurk,
Gently ghost whispers around the willow,
As a pale moon princess sitting, waiting,
The knight sees her and he feels warmth
As if he was safe, in love with her,
He approached slowly as if he'd been dazed by love,
Many whisper around her,
The knight begins to sink in the swamp of wailing death,
He shouts but no words come out,
The sky becomes blood-red,
Blood rushing through his veins as he didn't foresee
a princess of death,
As he sinks to a long endless sleep.

Ethan Spencer (15)
Hartsdown Technology College

Myself

As I walk the road
I look across and all I see
Is myself looking back at me.
He's lost,
I'm missing,
I can't find myself,
I'm not the person I want to be
I'm beaten, reduced to nothing,
My life is crushed beneath the ruins
I just want to be myself,
But I'm prevented by no-faced people,
I scream to myself to let me die,
I just look away to live my life.

Gerry Keavey (16)
Hartsdown Technology College

RIP Grandad

Oh Grandad, why did you have to leave us?
Must it have been so soon?
Oh Grandad, how you used to tell those jokes,
Making all the folks laugh.
Oh Grandad, what's it like in Heaven?
Kallum's nearly eleven.
Oh Grandad, how we miss you,
We'll never forget you.

Lauren Pulman (15)
Hartsdown Technology College

Bullying

Bullying is bad
But it still goes on,
It's like a tradition of causing pain, misery and upset,
It is an awful thing
Which many people partake in,
It hurts so many
But they're scared to do anything,
They hide instead,
If they feel fear, they are far too distant
For any man to reach
A nervous man stands instead.

Gareth Cole (16)
Hartsdown Technology College

I Wonder

I wonder what it would be like to be him,
The quiet person in the corner,
The boy with his back to the wall in the playground.

The child that no one knows his phone number,
He is the only one that comes to school with bruises on his face,
No one bullies him because they know nothing about him.

I wonder what it would be like to be him?
I wonder!

Daniel Pellegrini (13)
Hartsdown Technology College

Untitled

Do my eyes deceive me?
Does the wind whistle your name
Or am I still dreaming?

The clouds form shapes and what do I see?
It is you, it is me.
But I know we cannot be,
For I am not where you are.

My lonely heart beats only when the wind blows,
It echoes your name,
But I am foolish,
We died when I did.

Will I move on
Or am I forced to exist?
Limbo is the only place for me now.

Joe Perkins (16)
Hartsdown Technology College

Dreaming?

Lost.
Stranded on the border of reality and imagination.
Suspended in time
Hope and despair, truth and lies:
Melt into one.
A vicious circle
Unable to break free -
Thoughts continue to stream around:
The island of my mind.
Swirling, rushing, boundaries collide
Unable to control
These escaping emotions
Reality pulls me back
With a jolt.

Ella Dove (15)
Maidstone Grammar School for Girls

When A Girl

She no longer hears the ring of the bell;
Only the echo of her cries.

She looks up to see the fading light as a star dies
The clock hands are itching, ticking to be turned back
To before, when her hair shone and smelt of close nights,
When her eyes welcomed sleep and her hands were soft.
Now hardened from lies and harsh waters they write frantic
Poems
    Songs
        Love letters.

She can hear the ticking
But she still has more to lose.
More shattered words to piece together.
At 4.52 on a forgotten morning.

It's not her time yet
It's not even
    quarter
        to.

Kelsey Heard (15)
Maidstone Grammar School for Girls

Origins Of Beauty

Beauty is simply one word
But has so many meanings.
Beauty is like love
Comes from within and is part of everyone.
Beauty is not only seen,
Through wondering eyes of the world.
Beauty can have a taste
As well as a smell.
Beauty can often be touched
And never be fully appreciated.
Beauty can be a sound
That remains in a soul of another.
Beauty is small and simple
And lacks recognition.
Beauty is a newborn
Brought into the world.
Beauty is the old
When their time comes to an end.
Beauty comes from the heart
But is portrayed by the soul.

Natasha Mills (15)
Maidstone Grammar School for Girls

Lost In The Outback!

I'm lost, I'm all alone,
I'm all on my own.
I'm stuck in the outback
No home
No Aussies for miles and miles
Can't take it anymore
No sleep
No nothing for weeks, months, years
No care
No fear or false hope
That someone will come
No food
No survival skills to keep me alive
Not much longer now
Strange light coming towards me
Could it be Heaven or, no it's a vehicle.
I've been saved
Plenty of water
Here I come home, I'm not alone!

Catherine Roxborough-Barham (11)
Mascalls School

Deaf

Every morning when I wake, I do not hear a sound,
The thing that wakes me is not an alarm clock,
The thing that wakes me at the start is my trusty hound.
When my family call me, I do not hear the phone,
When my family ring, I don't hear a thing
When my hound taps my leg, I feel it right to the bone,
I say write me a letter to say what you must say,
They may reply, they may not,
All I know is I get a letter every day.
At school I struggled, being deaf it was hard for me,
It was hard for me, but now it is easy,
Now everything's easy and every day just brings glee.

Jack Panteney-Lyttle (12)
Mascalls School

Christmas Is Near

Christmas is near,
What's that I hear?
Santa's sleigh?
Hip hip hooray!

Sitting by the fire,
All snuggled up,
I really do admire,
Roast turkey dinner.

Carol singers at the door,
Singing Silent Night
I listen to another four
Then I fall asleep.

Wake up on Christmas morning
Look out of the window and start yawning
There it is
All the snow
The one thing I've been dreaming
Christmas is here.

David Perry (11)
Mascalls School

What Will It Be Like In The Future?

In the future,
There might be one-eyed creatures
And people that have three ears.

In the future,
There could be lots of vultures,
Circling around in space.

There could be,
Robots that look like me,
There might be flowers that grow in the sea.

There could be,
Animals that love the taste of tea
Or people that like to be stung by a bee.

But that is only what I think
And I'm sure you're thinking of something else.

Kathryn Lawson-Wood (11)
Mascalls School

A Goth's Point Of View

Everyone says goths are bad people
They also say we're lethal.
They say we vandalise the towns and take drugs
Just 'cause we wear dark clothes and like the Devil, Hell.

All my friends are goths like me
They don't have ASBOs or get involved with the police
I don't see why the papers never listen to our point of view
All they say are 'Goths are this' and 'Grungers are that'.

The government never let us have a word
Like I said they won't let us speak
They talk for us, we're alienated people, can't you see?

Alex Wood (11)
Mascalls School

On My Own

The dark dusty alley
The bright full moon
Looking round for shelter
But night's come too soon.

People are awakening
Getting out of bed
Whilst I'm stuck here
In this dirty old shed.

Warm on the outside
Cold on the in
Searching for a scrap of food
In anyone's bin.

I need someone who loves me
Some family or friend
But no one's here beside me
Alone in Crouch End.

No one wants to know me
No one even cares
I bottle up emotions
Whilst creeping up their stairs.

They're sleeping in the bedroom
All snug, cosy and tight
They don't know I'm out here
Shivering with fright.

Georgia Young (12)
Mascalls School

Mates

If I had to say the troubles in the world,
The people dying and the hard solid woes
Maybe I wouldn't start with the bad news
I would keep on going to what may abuse
The people who cry at night
And the people who have joy
'Cause what life brings up are life's little joys.

The only reason life is good
Is because your mates are amazing like they should
They're always there, no matter what
Because whatever they do, they just don't stop . . .

Being your mate it's what they do
But when you lose them it's something new
Because all your life you've had your friend
Every step of the way, it's your life they mend.

Glen Gostlow (13)
Mascalls School

Hallowe'en

On the 31st October
Every child from Whitehurst Lane
Scatters the road from start to end.

Begging at the door
Their little feet on the floor
Sweets piled up in witch cauldrons
And no healthy things in sight.

Some faces are scary
Others are hairy
Some costumes are plain
Others are detailed and different.

On the 31st October
Every child from Whitehurst Lane
Scatters the road from start to end.

Amy Broad (12)
Mascalls School

Stars

Stars are born
Stars twinkle
Stars smile
Stars laugh
Stars sparkle.

They live in the sky
They're seen in your eye
They're not a star shape
They aren't stars as we think
They are bits of rock.

Are they real?
Are they there?
Are they the stars that make the sky?
Are they golden?
Are they yellow?

Roofs block out the starry view
Rays of stars seen at night
Rich golden or rich yellow
Rays of stars so bright.

Stars light up the world
Smiling stars all night
Stars are living
Stars cry out
Stars die out.

Becky Beeching (12)
Mascalls School

A Chimney Boy's Woe

Tonight's the night I'm back on the streets
All I do is sweep, sweep, sweep.
Bad, not good, not lovely for sure
Perhaps my pain God will cure
I try and try to be good
I'd cry and cry, if only I could.

Here I am in the streets
Trying to cry, weep, weep, weep.
My mother left me long ago
My dad walked away, I shouted, 'No!'
Even though my heart's full of woe
I try and try not to, not to cry.

Laurie Taylor (12)
Mascalls School

The Vampires

Their skin gets paler by the day,
Those that walk the murderous way.
Their red eyes darken in the night
Endlessly searching for a neck to bite.

Their pointed fangs sparkle in the moonlight,
Cloaks flapping in the wind like kites
As they scale the walls of a silent house,
As fast as a cheetah, as quiet as a mouse.

The vein was pulsing in her neck,
He was ready to send another into death.
He knew he had done some terrible deeds,
But that's the only way the vampire feeds!

Ellie Hazell (13)
Mascalls School

Why?

I want to know why this was done to me?
I need to know why I couldn't see
You left me on my own
You never heard me moan
So why did you do this to me?

You've done things you shouldn't
You took things I couldn't
So why did you do this to me?
You loved him, he left
You weren't your best.

I tried and tried
But all you did was hide
Now I'm not there, you don't seem to care
So why did you do this to me?
At home you never seem to be there.

When you're at home
You're never on the phone
I call and I call
But you never answer
So why did you do this to me?

All I want is a chat
I really don't know
How to get you to understand
Why I went and what I did
I didn't mean to hurt you.

Kate Boughton (12)
Mascalls School

What Happens If . . . ?

What happens if I was being bullied?
My life, worth as much as one penny.
How could I contain that fear?
Would I ever end the crisis?

My life mashed up like mashed potato
All my happiness, hiding, hiding from me.

What happens if I was the bully?
Acting all strong and brave
Every day, every minute
Teasing someone small, someone scared
But really, deep down,
I am weak and I am hurt
But I don't want to show it, no never.

Katie Kneller (12)
Mascalls School

My Favourite Things

Red is my favourite colour
It reminds me of strawberry sauce.
My favourite person is my grandad
He has two puppies that are very funny.
They always chase me.
My grandad's garden is a paradise
With a small wood and a slide
I have so much fun.
My favourite drink is Coca-Cola
It gives me a tickling feeling.
I really love pasta and cheese
I eat it so quick my mum goes, 'Wow-wee!'
My favourite teddy is my Gromit
From Wallace and Gromit
And whenever we have a storm I cuddle him.

Luke Hall (11)
Mascalls School

My Favourite Things

I like the colour blue
As blue as the sky maybe
Or the blue cold sea rushing up the beach
As long as the water doesn't touch my feet.

I like being with Katie
Who is my next-door neighbour
She's kind and funny
But sometimes very annoying.

I lay on the trampoline
And look up at the sky
I look at the clouds
And guess what they could be.

I like the soft ginger hair
Of my favourite cat
Also the black velvet cat
Which always likes a cuddle.

Bethany Hunt (11)
Mascalls School

My Favourite Things

My favourite colour is dark ocean blue,
Crashing, splashing onto the hard stones.
It reminds me of my friends and family
Having fun and running round.

Staring into the ocean I see a reflection of me
My favourite person is Shannen Grainge
Because she makes me feel all happy again.
Also in the ocean I see my family all smiling at me
The sun is blazing down on me
Melting chocolate ready for me after tea.

Jessica Wells (11)
Mascalls School

My Favourite Things

I've got loads of favourite things,
My room is packed full of them.
My favourite colour is red
Shining in my eyes from my Man U top.
I like R&B music the best
Blasting through my stereo speakers, full blast.
One of my best mates is Miles,
He makes me laugh so much
When he does something stupid.
I like Lucozade Sport
The energy goes through me like a red arrow
My best piece of clothing is my Man U top
I like the feeling of being really happy and excited
Like when Christmas is here.

Jack Budd (11)
Mascalls School

My Favourite Things

I have so many favourite things
They make me feel so happy
Strawberry milkshake
With cream on top would be my best drink.

I have loads of CDs but mostly pop
And if I had a choice of colours
It would be light glittery blue.

My favourite emotion would be
When I'm sitting down by a fireplace
When it's pouring down with rain
Chicken (spicy) fajitas
The most delicious food ever.

So many things I love so much
But the best thing ever
Would be living with my mum and dad
Safe and sound.

Soothing blue, the best colour
On my pictures on the wall
I feel so calm when I paint this colour
That's all of my favourite things
I think I will have more to come.

Harriet Biggs (11)
Mascalls School

My Feelings

Pink is my colour, like petals from a rose,
I love the feel of white cotton tinkling on my toes.
My favourite place is under the sun
Although I love to cuddle my mum.
I love the feel of snowflakes
And drinking ice-cold strawberry milkshakes.
The feeling of sitting by the fire
Oh that's my desire.
The sound of birds in the morning,
It really stops me from yawning.
Being happy is my emotion,
I love the feel of soft bubbly body lotion.
I have my many favourite feelings
From all different emotions
They come and go
Like waves in the ocean!

Alexandra Williams (11)
Mascalls School

My Favourite Things

I have many favourite things
Somehow they remind me how special I am
Watching Man United on the TV
Hoping they will win the cup
Hoping that I will play for them some day
I will be very happy
Favourite player of the team is
Edwin van der Sar
He is the goalkeeper for Man United
I hope some day that I could take his place.

Louis Still (12)
Mascalls School

My Favourite Things

My favourite thing is . . .

The heavy roar of heavy metal
The constant drumming of my favourite songs
The scream of the lyrics shouting out
An echo from the full crowd.

The high screech from the guitar
Boom! Boom! goes the big bass drum
The low sound of the bass guitar
That's why I like heavy metal!

Louis Ayre (11)
Mascalls School

My Favourite Things

I have many favourite things
I feel special when I play with my drums
Because it relaxes me and I can release my anger
The red on my drums makes me glow like the moon in the sky
When I put heavy metal on, it makes me happy
It makes me want to move.

Adam Foster (11)
Mascalls School

Favourite Things

I have many favourite things
They all make me feel safe.

My favourite food is chocolate gateaux
I always feel safe when I am snuggling under my bed covers
And looking at my favourite colour violet
It makes me think of flowers and when I am with my mum.

I think music always calms me down
And also when I am in my bedroom in my silky pyjamas.

My favourite music is pop, I like listening to Britney Spears
I have many favourite things
They all make me feel safe.

Hope Timson (12)
Mascalls School

Untitled

Round about the ring I go
Flying punches to and fro
Knocking my opponent to the floor
Booing fans getting bored
Training hard to get fit
Trainer's not giving me time to sit.

Happy when I win
Opponent kicks me on my shin
I give him a right hook
The crowd stop and look
Finally I've got time to rest
Better train to be the best.

Peter Ryder (12)
Mascalls School

Homeless

A person walking, wandering the streets, lonely and cold with
                                         nowhere to live
H aving to search through rubbish to try and find something to eat
O bviously having no money to buy a thing
M outhing water from a birdbath
E verywhere he goes he hears laughing
L osing the will to live
E nding up wearing second-hand clothes
S leeping on a bed of rags
S imply wishing for more of a chance

P erhaps someone would give him a home
E xplaining that he needs better
R obyn was that soul willing to give him shelter
S oon getting a job and clothes
O n his way to recovery
N ow Tom is happy having got a home.

He is happy, but what about the next person?

Matthew Stace (11)
Mascalls School

Why?

Why is the sky blue?
Why are you, you?
Why is the Earth round?
How come there is sound?

These are all questions
And I want answers
Give me them now!

Why is day, day?
Why is there May?
Why is there a night?
Why do we have sight?

These are all questions
And I want answers
Give me them now!

Give me them . . . *please*
Please
Please.

James Richardson (11)
Mascalls School

Homeless Child

What would it feel like to be a homeless child?
Nothing to eat, nothing to share
How could you live off scraps and rubbish?
No one will share, no one will care
But don't worry, help is at hand.
The rest of the nation must surely give
To help a young child to learn how to live.
How could a child live off the bare little?
A ready-made meal is rare to find
So why can't someone be kind?
He is alone
Won't someone give him a home?
How can you be a homeless child?

Thomas Price (11)
Mascalls School

Alex

I like Alex
She is funny
She's beautiful
That's why I like her.

I like Alex
She is very *loud*
She is wicked
That's why I like her.

I like Alex
She has hazel eyes
And brunette hair
That's why I like her.

I like Alex
She is cool
She is pretty
That's why I like her.

I like Alex
She is very weird
And very rich
That's the way she is.

Vicki Loader (12)
Mascalls School

A Lonely Spirit

A lonely spirit, a spectre, a wisp
This lonely ghost only had one wish
To never be lonely and have a friend
But he has a heart that will never mend.

As his heart wanders in despair
The day will end shortly and no one will care
As the love bleeds, like water it flows
The lonely spirit wanders as its hope may not glow.

Charles Monk (12)
Mascalls School

Horses!

I have lots of favourite things like:
Down at the stables having so much fun
Soaring over jumps in the bright yellow sun
Sitting in the saddle for hours on end
Weaving and bending
I feel freedom with the wind blowing in my hair
Wandering where we want like a pair
I feel so special to be on his back
He is a good little chap
Wandering together out of sight
Maybe we'll be gone all night.

Rebecca Napper (11)
Mascalls School

My Favourite Things

I have many favourite things
It makes me feel special.
My favourite colour is sky-blue
I hope that's yours too.
I'm into rapping
50 Cent and Chris Brown too.

I have many favourite things
It makes me feel special.
My hobby is to play football
It's my ambition to become
Professional and I won't give up my dream.

Ryan Cornelius (11)
Mascalls School

Football Teams

F ootballs going in the net
O ranges at half-time
O ver the crossbar into the crowd
T oo low, hear them cheering loud
B lue, the colour of my boots
A ll alone he shoots
L ovely shot in the corner
L ook at him, he's a brilliant scorer

T hey've won the Cup
E very shot on target
A well-deserved goal in the net
M any bad tackles, the whistle goes
S ent off and that's the end!
    Football teams!

Jack Cummins (11)
Mascalls School

My Dog Dylan

I love my dog Dylan
Like I love my family
He is a boxer
And loves to be naughty
He runs round the garden like a loony
Doing his laps
He has a black wet nose
With white on the outside
He has black around his eyes and black ears
He has ginger on the rest
He has a little stubby tail
That wags when I get home from school
He is as soft as silk
When he hugs me
And falls asleep on my lap.

Megan Wills (11)
Mascalls School

My Favourite Things

Blue is my colour
It is the deep blue of the wide shimmering ocean
Calming and tranquil.

Zante in Greece is my favourite place
The golden sands are like a lady's fair skin
The sea shimmers like a shower of diamonds.

Love is my favourite feeling
I feel happy when wrapped in my mum's arms
I feel safe, secure and loved.

Ice cream float is my favourite drink
The fizzy soda bubbles floating in the air
The ice cream is crisp and cold, like a winter's morning.

Christopher Lively (12)
Mascalls School

My Favourite Things

My favourite things, I have many
Yellow is the colour, the colour of the sun
Listening to music makes me tap the beat
Thinking of cheese melting on my pasta
The snow comes down and the lights go on
I'm really happy that Christmas has come
Opening presents makes me really happy
Come on Mum, make it snappy!

Harriet Entwistle (11)
Mascalls School

My Bedroom

M ountains of cosy cushions
Y ellow as bright as the sun

B ed as comfy as the clouds
E ndless sleep
D ancing around in my dreams
R ushing around in the world of slumber
O n goes the music
O ver and over again
M unching of popcorn with my friends.

Shelley Frankling (11)
Mascalls School

The Arctic

The white snow surrounds me in the Arctic world
The layout looks so simple and silent
Like the grains of snow that fall
This is the land of tranquillity
That is to be ruined in days to come
The tranquillity will melt away
The simplicity will fade.

Will Jeffery (12)
Mascalls School

The Lion

I'm moving through the grass
Slowly, silently, alone
I think to myself, *I must catch my dinner*
And I've got to do it for my family as well.

There it is!
My dinner!
It's just a small warthog
But it's good enough for me.

I race to catch it
Or my family will starve
I take off with my back legs
Bang! the deed is done.

Oh no, here comes its mum
Oh well, I guess it will be two for the price of one!

I bring back the meat
My family tuck in
I am proud that I've done it
I am glad that we won't starve.

Alex Neale (11)
Mascalls School

The Future

The future is great, the future is fun
You can do what you want, whenever you want
No bedtime unless you want to
Eating food whenever you want
Can't you believe or can you believe?
But I can believe, can you?

The future is cool
New things to see wherever you go
New people to see
New animals to see
In the future a cheetah is slow and an elephant is fast
In the future anything can happen
But can you believe? Can you believe?
But I can believe, can you?

In the future it is not so good
The schools are gone, so you don't learn much
Your parents are gone, so really you don't have fun
It's quite fun but you all need your family to be a family
So all I can say is don't always think you are better
Without a family believe me it's not fun
So trust me, now you can believe.

Jack Richardson (11)
Mascalls School

I'm Alone

I sit at home alone
I sit on the sofa all snuggled up
I feel all lonely because no one is there to play with me
I sit here and purr with boredom
I want someone there with me to play or at least something
Because I sit at home alone, on the sofa, snuggled up.

Chelsea Clift (12)
Mascalls School

Paint A Picture

Paint a picture of a fierce tiger
Ready to pounce and catch its prey
Its bright, red, hollow eyes stare at you so deeply
Never wanting to interfere!

Paint a picture of best friends
Happily playing as good friends do
Sleepovers, make-up and midnight feasts
No time for dinner!

Paint a picture of a gigantic chocolate bar
All yummy, thick and chunky to bite into
Licking my lips and eating away
'Too nice to stop,' as I say!

Lauren Sears (11)
Mascalls School

My Twin

When midnight is here
I crawl in my bed
'Mummy, Mummy.'
That is what I said.

When I shut my eyes
I see a new world
A world white as snow
Help me Mummy
I just want to go.

I look around and what can I see
In the distance, I see someone like me.

I walk, I run
But he's still miles away
Who was that boy?
He's running away.

I open my eyes
And what can I see
Someone sitting, right next to me
Someone who looks, just like me.

Edward Weaver-Coles (11)
Mascalls School

Just A Moment

When a moment strikes
It can feel harder than daggers
But thinking back on it
Can't even compare.

The sorrow spreads forth
Like a burning fire destroying all hope
You're hoping it'll go
But you know all too well.

When a moment strikes
It can feel harder than daggers
But thinking back on it
Can't even compare.

Gabrielle Brown (12)
Mascalls School

The Lonely And The Disabled

How can people cope without any hope?
Some people can't walk or can't even talk.
Sometimes I wonder if I was alone
Sleeping in the streets and without a home
I wish the world was a better place
A kinder place and a sweeter place
I wish people would look at the disabled
As they would look at me.

Thomas Weaver-Coles (11)
Mascalls School

My Midnight Visitor

If I tell you this, you promise not to tell?
It's all about my visitor that always comes at twelve.
When I see the black cloak emerge, I hide under my bed
And watch for those frail bony feet.

The blood drips out and spreads across my floor
Staining the carpet like red wine!
A hand with two severed fingers crawls out into the thick dusty air.

Never knowing when to breathe, I lay still, petrified and scared
But this isn't the end of it, there's much, much more to come
The next thing I see dropped on the floor is a fleshy, broken thumb.

I slowly see the kneecaps bend and crouch down is what it does
Squeezing pus and making squeaks
A liver drops out the front.

As it rests upon its arm, it snaps off letting out a wild shriek,
It flops down next to me staring into my eyes
Those big, hanging-out eyes
Just hanging on by one weak muscle!

I finally get the courage to move and roll straight through . . .
My midnight visitor!

Sharna Marks (11)
Mascalls School

It's Hard To Be Blind

It's hard to be blind, no one cares or minds
What you think or do
All you can do is think and listen
Think and listen, just what to do.
It's hard to be blind, you have to be signed
On to a list and look after yourself
You have to listen to know what to do
And have someone or something to help you along
It's hard to be blind, it's like a dog with no legs
A sheep with no baa, a mind that's been tied up
In chains all because you're blind.
It's hard to be blind, you are different
Different in ways, like you have to read Braille
And have a dog or a stick.
It's hard to be blind, you have special needs
Like special books, special sticks, even special glasses
I hate to be special, in a different way
Just because I'm blind.

Kelly Moran (12)
Mascalls School

Africa

Not knowing better
Tired and lonely
Not even knowing
Help is at hand.

Resting after
A long day of work
Not even knowing
Help is at hand.

Some may be hungry
But happy inside
How would they know
What's better in life?

The poor and homeless
Walking the streets
How would they know
What's better in life?

Thankful and friendly
Emotions running wild
'Help me please,'
Says a small child.

Wondering what's happening out there,
'Help me please,'
Says a small child.

But all in all
What do they know
Help is at hand
But surely they know
Don't you think so?

Amy Roberts (12)
Mascalls School

The Solar System

Imagine stepping into the shuttle
Saying goodbye to the ones you love
As the rocket launches into space
Up to the stars above.

Imagine soaring through outer space
Zooming past the stars
Past Mercury, Venus, Planet Earth
And bright red Mars.

Let's move onto Jupiter
And maybe Saturn too
As you fly past Uranus
You might see something new.

Only two more planets left
Very different in size
As you soar past Neptune
You won't believe your eyes.

Back into the asteroid belt
Back to Earth soon
Whenever you look into the sky
You'll think of your trip past the moon.

Amy Couchman (11)
Mascalls School

African Kid

A frica is my home
F riends I do not have, I'm all alone
R eally there are no phones
I think my father has passed away
C ould he come back to me
A nother night without any tea

N ever have I had sweets
E very night I cry myself to sleep
E ven I lie in a heap
D reaming that I have friends and food

O h I wish I had food
U ntil I am old enough to have a job
R eally I just have to sob

H ow I need the money to survive
E motions are all mixed
L eaking roof on hut needs to be fixed
P eople don't care at all

F ierce things around, I could get hurt
O h, no one cares, do they?
O h, if they were in my shoes right now
D o they know what it's like?

W ater is all murky in the mud
A nother day, no shoes
T he ground is wet, my feet are sinking
E veryone looks at me
R eally not, they just look through me

M um, Dad, I don't have them
O h, do they care at all?
N o one ever listens
E yes watch me in my sleep
Y es, oh why me?

Shelley Manser (11)
Mascalls School

Blind

Are you happy, are you sad?
Are you kind or are you bad?
Do you know this, are you mad?
These are the questions that haunt me!

Are you tall?
Are you small?
Can you feel it when you fall?
Have you ever fallen from a tree?

You cannot see but you can hear!
Therefore you should show no fear!
Never ever shed a tear
Be proud that you can hear, you just can't see.

Rhys Gray (12)
Mascalls School

The Tiger

I prowl through the jungle,
I prowl through the trees
I am king of the jungle
And everyone's proud of me.

The jungle is great, the jungle is grand
And all the animals prance around
They all have friends apart from me
Because I'm scary as you can see.

I creep through the jungle
I creep through the trees
Looking for somebody
To be there for me.

I need someone there when I am scared
To help me through the darkness
But I can't . . . why me?
Why me?

Kate Sparkhall (11)
Mascalls School

Arsenal

Arsenal, Arsenal, I support you
My favourite player is Thierry Henry, he is my idol
Arsenal, I will support you though the bad and good
I want to play for you I think I should
Even though I am not that good.

Arsenal, Arsenal, you're very wise
You know who to substitute when you look to the skies
You got them to the final in the Champions League
When I found out, I was so pleased.

Roberto Scaramastra (12)
Mascalls School

Untitled

Sitting here in my room
Feeling rather in the gloom
Gazing up to the stars trying to see
The wonderful things life can be.

Oh my goodness, what's that?
It's black, big and shaped like a hat
Shooting down, blazing bright
Really what is it? I'm getting a fright.

Getting larger and bigger, brighter too
What is it really, a present from you?
Now I'm lying here in the dust
Covered by a horrible musk.

It turns out now
That burning bright
In the silent night
Was a planet shining with all its might.

Zoë Powell (13)
Mascalls School

London

Pickpockets walking around, looking for food
The sound of horseshoes on the gravel
Rings through the town's streets
Market holders shouting and selling their goods

Then the morning sun glistening off Buckingham Palace
Watching over big, busy London
Plus the hustle and bustle, Piccadilly Circus
With Big Ben ringing in the distance
And London Eye spinning silently round
Then across the Thames, Tower of London stands alone
But then look around then look down
And think what's underground?

Then look to the future and see all the sights
Prince William, King
Then quite a big shock
As hover cars fly across all the streets
But now London's bigger, what happens next?

Sarah Loines (12)
Mascalls School

Outside I See

Outside I see
People playing in the tree
All the birds singing
Whilst all the children are swinging.

All I hear
Is the cheer
Of all their friends.

I can't wait
To see them again
To share the excitement
Once again.

Bethany Wright (11)
Mascalls School

Blind Man

It's horrible, not being able to see,
You don't know what anyone looks like,
Or if you want to choose some clothes,
How do you know what colour you like?
Of if you want to watch a film,
How can you see the drama?
Or maybe if you want to learn to drive,
'How can you, you can't see?' they'd say.
But I have a friend, a friend that cares
That friend is my guide dog
Yes, that friend is my guide dog!

Emily Medcalf (11)
Mascalls School

I Am Unique

I am unique in my own special way
I show this to people step by step each day.
People like me because of my personality
It's not on the outside they look
It's on the inside like the words in a book.
I like to sing my heart out
Like a kettle with a spout
It tells you when it's done
But I sing purely for fun.
I am very much like my mother
But as you know everyone is different from each other
I live in Paddock Wood
But I really wish I could
Live right beside a pier
In the heart of Yorkshire.
When I go to sleep at night
I purely dream about
The day I pass my A-Levels
In my dreams I have no doubts!

Amie Barrett (11)
Mascalls School

Unique

You're not the same as me
No one can be
I am unique and happy to be me
I like to ride and play with my friends
You can always see different trends
No one can be the same as anyone else
So just be yourself and not anyone else
Just be yourself because you are unique.

Abbie Fuller (11)
Mascalls School

My Family

I am not a girly girl,
A pinky girl, a purple girl
But I am a blue and green
One with marvellous, wonderful dreams.

He likes lager,
He likes beer
He likes wearing his fishing gear
He likes travelling on his bike
But he doesn't like singing with a mic
He likes to kayak on the river
He likes snakes that slither, slither.

Mum has short brown hair
She's like a cuddly bear
She loves ice cream
Lots and lots
She likes flowers that grow in pots.

That is my family
Lucky me!

Lauren Cox (12)
Mascalls School

Alienation

A ll alone, no one to hold me
L iving my life by myself
I n the playground I just lie around
E nglish class I sit by myself
N ow I've moved school I have no one to hold me
A round the world no one can be suffering as much as me
T hrough other people's eyes I see hope and a life worth living
I n my eyes, it's dull, grey and dismal
O n the way home I get beaten up
N o one to hold me.

Kieron Pattenden (12)
Mascalls School

Never Be Lonely

Sitting all alone here
In my own style
Won't anyone notice me
Make me laugh and smile?

Come on over here please
Just a little while
A little bit of love please
Make me laugh and smile.

Here comes a friendly face
We have the same sort of style
Could he be the one for me
Make me laugh and smile?

I've never felt like this
Not by a mile
Am I just dreaming
Make me laugh and smile?

Here comes someone else
She took a little while
Then told him to leave me
Make me laugh and smile.

Dreaming you can buy now
A whole life free of trial
This boy is my reality
He makes me laugh and smile.

Kerrie Chamberlain (11)
Mascalls School

The Lazy Dog

Every morning I wake up to play
Another game, another day
Every morning I go for a walk
Where all the humans do a talk.

Then I come back for something to eat
There it is, all nice and sweet
Then I lay by the fire, all nice and warm
And sleep and dream until it is dawn.

Then I wake up for another day
Where all I do is sleep and play.

Brad Garrett (11)
Mascalls School

Majestic Mammals

Lions

L ions are fierce animals
I f you tried to stroke one it would bite you
O n a lion's good day it would just scratch you
N o is the answer to stroking lions!

Tigers

T igers are beautiful animals
I n the wild they roam
G oing past trees and trees as he lurks
E ven though the poachers wait
R eady to make their move
S o the tiger lurks to wait for his move.

Panther

P ouncing around all day long
A ll they do is pounce along
N ever ever calm
T ails like swords, long and smooth
H air as soft as sponges
E bony silk are their coats
R eady to pounce, pounce, pounce.

Alec Fleming (11)
Mascalls School

A Thought Of Ghosts

Would you like to be a ghost
And not know what it's like
To be totally ignored
For the rest of your life?

They scare us, yet they give us company
But are they all just all in our head?
They make us laugh, they make us cry
And scare us in our beds.

Are they real or are the not?
Is it a personal choice?
Can they move objects
And can they use their voice?

It must be lonely and sad and scary
Or maybe they are evil or even friendly
Love them alive whilst they are still here
Love them truly and love them tenderly.

Charlotte Whiting-Searle (12)
Mascalls School

That Day

I will always remember that day
That day my father left
The 6th of March 2004
Struggling at a gym competition
Whilst he packed his bags
He let me and my brothers down
Days later realised what's happening
We thought he had no heart
About three months later we had news
My father wanted contact.

People talked me into it
I was scared, nervous, but happy too
The day came, but I didn't want to go
I went in, I was shocked
My dad was there with his girlfriend Lynne
He was different and much bigger
Didn't have much hair either
I didn't really know what to think
He started talking, his voice was deeper.

I started to visit regularly
Doing different things each time we met
Was loving him again
One summer I stayed at his house
It was great, we went shopping daily
We bought loads of great stuff
I don't like having to say goodbye
Counting days till I see him again
Love going to see him
I am so glad we are getting on
But I will always remember that day.

Chloe Marsh (11)
Mascalls School

The Cruellest Thing

As time has gone,
The matters have worsened,
Arguments have increased
And everything seems burdened.

Life feels like war,
Easy to start and hard to finish,
Every time it comes up,
I wish it would vanish.

Here in my room
I lay unsettled,
Watching the day come and go,
Leaving all my thoughts nothing but bedazzled.

My face has been scarred as well as my life,
Yet from all that has happened,
I still feel the pain,
Of being strangled and threatened each and every night.

This streak of evilness has struck my heart
As I ask one question only,
Why, why I am being torn apart?
Why is it I feel exceedingly lonely?

I wish to depart myself from this life,
But wonder whether it is normal,
For someone to experience such lowlife
Being treated in the most unreal, vile way!

Rikah Louie (13)
Northfleet School for Girls

Bullying

B ullying is a boy thing
U nderstand bullies and stamp them out
L ike everyone
L ittle children crying every day
Y ou do not want this
I do not want this
N ow bullies have lost
G iven us the strength to stand up to bullies.

Mary Wilkie (12)
Pent Valley Technology College

Living In A World Of Sounds

I hear the plane high in the sky
I hear the birds outside close by
I hear the wind blowing the trees
I hear the change rattling by my knees
I hear the people loud in the crowd
I hear the car brakes screeching so loud
I hear the dog going, *ruff, ruff, ruff*
I see . . . nothing.

Class S4 (15-16)
St Nicholas School for Children with Learning Difficulties, Canterbury

It Has To Be Told . . .

My best friend's eyes glisten like the shiniest ever jewel
Her skin is pure and milky white like the white from a toadstool.
Her hair is dark with streaks of blonde that glitter like the sun
She is very quiet and does not shout and loves being round her mum.
Sometimes if you ask her something, she'll nod her head or shake
And very rarely she turns her eyes into that position you'd find

on a snake.

The kids, they bully her, but no matter what, I'm there
Sometimes I give them evils (a horrid type of stare).
We stick together like Siamese twins or PVA glue
And if my friend wants to do something, I will do it too.
My friend, I know, is very quiet, but I can understand that
My friend can't talk and I can't hear
Why can't anyone buy that?

Finley Clark (11)
The Abbey School

If Only I Could Talk

If only I could talk
I would tell them about . . .
My mate Red
He cut his leg on broken glass
It got infected, he couldn't hunt so he died.

If only I could talk
I would tell them about . . .
The swan who swallowed fishing line
If it wasn't for the RSPCA he would have died.

If only I could talk
I would tell them about . . .
The hedgehog who got his head stuck in a baked bean tin
He couldn't eat - he died of starvation.

If only I could talk
I would tell them about . . .
The small animals who lost their homes when the sun
Shining through a discarded bottle, set the forest on fire.

If only I could talk
I would tell them that . . .
I worry about my cubs when they go out
That they might pick up something that may harm them.

If only I could talk
I would tell them about . . .
The dangers of dropping litter in our countryside.

Joseph Ellett (11)
The Abbey School

The Unsaid

Deep inside a human's throat lies a voice
A voice that has not yet spoken
The words from a dictionary, they're no use
The words from your heart remain unsaid
The voice inside remains quite dead
The voice in my head screams instead,
'Won't someone listen to what I've said?'

Nikijay Spicer (11)
The Abbey School

To Give A Voice To Someone Who Can't Speak

It must be horrible to not be able to speak
Just feeling very, very weak.
Only being able to eat a pear
Without people starting to look and stare.
As they point at the door
And people giggling at the floor.
Whether depressed, dumb or gay
Everyone should have a say.

James Keen (12)
The Abbey School

The Boy Who Couldn't Speak

There was a boy who couldn't speak
So he tried to read my lips
His way to communicate
Is his hands and fingertips.

If everyone learned to sign
It would help this person out
He is not like most of us
Unable to scream and shout.

He points to this and points to that
In the hope we understand
If we all did our little bit
His life would be more grand.

Ryan Beake (11)
The Abbey School

Give Me A Voice

It all started a month ago something really scary
But since then I haven't spoken
Because it's really scared me.

I haven't spoken to anyone, I've ignored them completely
But I feel really bad
But it's not my fault really.

Everywhere I go they stare at me
I overhear them and they say,
'Look there, it's the girl who lost her voice, isn't it freaky?'

When I go home my brother says to me,
'Ellie, Ellie, it's OK, you can talk to me.'

I was just about to open my mouth then my mum walked in,
'Max! Max! has it worked yet?'
'No, she was just about so speak
Then you charged in now she's shut her mouth completely.'

When Mum left he tried again, 'Ellie, Ellie, talk to me please?'
'Max?'
'Yes, Ellie.'
'I've seen something.'
'What Ellie?'
'I've seen a murder.'

Abbi Coe (11)
The Abbey School

I Can't Speak For A Reason

It's always hard when you're a boy that likes men
It's always hard to tell people
Maybe no one will listen
Maybe no one cares
You might not talk because of it
You might be ashamed
But don't let it put you down
Be proud
Be proud
Be gay and proud.

Tania Murray (11)
The Abbey School

Away With Words

To you, you know no different
Your fingers are your voice
We sit and talk together
And you teach me your language
We laugh together as I get it wrong
Your fingers go faster the more we laugh
I understand you
But you don't understand me
I will keep trying
And you will keep helping
Because at the end of the day
We are best friends
Who don't need words.

Aaron Munns (11)
The Abbey School

The Voice

Who will speak for me now I am no longer?
There he lies in the cold, dark earth
Who will speak for him now he is no longer here?
The worms will speak
The birds will tweet
The leaves will flutter
And sigh as they fall
The sun will laugh and dance above the sky
As the clouds flutter by
The rain will groan
And the wind will moan
So he has no need to speak.

Hannah Woodfine (12)
The Abbey School

The Man Who Could Not Speak

As I walked past
Children would stare
But it didn't matter
Because I didn't care.

The children used to make fun of me
But I thought to myself, *at least I can see.*

As I got older
My confidence grew
My voice started to get louder
And I got prouder.

But now I speak and no one can stare
Because I'm as important as anyone there.

Jilly Taylor (11)
The Abbey School

I Wish I Could Speak

S ilence is what we are good at
I t is what we do
L ook and listen is all we can do
E veryone ignores us
N No one can make me hear
C an't speak a word
E veryone else can speak.

Jamie Smith (11)
The Abbey School

Silence Is Hard

Silence is hard
I have a secret I can't tell
Loudly I speak in my head
I can't speak; otherwise I will say it out loud
No one to speak to
Can't say a word as I will spit it out
Even trying to speak to a paper friend.

I can't
Still I can't speak even though the secret's gone
Having to do sign language
All the time
Reading is the only thing I can do
And does anyone have a voice for me?

Alice Mackrill (11)
The Abbey School

Silence

Silence is a cruel thing
That ruins people's lives
They have to learn sign language
Which is very, very hard.

I once had a deaf friend
She was really, really kind
She tried to talk to me
But I could not understand.

So I taught her the alphabet
And showed her how to write
And now she can write
Talk to me whenever she likes.

Emily Easter (11)
The Abbey School

Can't Speak

Sign language is hard
People ignore me
Listening seems easy
Education is important
Never talk again
Can't speak
Everyone speaks around me
Language seems hard
Speech is everything
Everyone ignores me
Voice has gone
Everyone stares at me
Reading is impossible
You talk to me but I can't talk back
Talking is something I can't do
Ha-ha, people say when I cannot reply
I can't speak.

Edward Gregory (11)
The Abbey School

Silence Is Mine

S o quiet
I wish I could speak
L ost my voice when I was born
E verybody is so loud
N othing to say
C an't tell anybody my problems
E very day I try to say something, but it's just not there

I wish I could go back in time
S ign language is hard to learn

M y family can all speak
I n school with people who can speak makes me feel bad
N ever been able to say anything, never will
E ven though I can't speak, I can still have a good life.

Gabrielle Henderson (11)
The Abbey School

The Man Who Lost His Voice

There once was a man
A nice man who loved football
But then an evil spirit came and took his voice
There could be only one thing he could do
He would have to help people who needed love
So every day he would give someone
In need of a voice and love
Everywhere he went he wished he could speak again
Then he got his voice back because he loved and helped.

Jack Crittenden (11)
The Abbey School

Can't Speak, Silence Is Boring!

C ommunication is what you need in life,
A bility to speak,
N ot for me though
T hings are boring without being able to speak

S peaking is all I dream of
P eople around me are always doing it
E veryone
A nywhere
K elly is the same as me, we can't speak

S ilence is boring
I llustrations are all I can communicate with
L istening is all right I suppose
E ducation is important
N othing is unimportant in life
C ommunication is the most important
E ven illustrations are hard to communicate with

I gnorance is annoying
S ign language is really hard

B e friends with everyone
O r even best friends
R eality is the best thing of life
I think I should get a speaking box
N ow that would be great
G reat! Then everyone would be able to hear me speak, wonderful!

Philip Epps (12)
The Abbey School

The Girl That Can't Speak

C all a friend
A nd let them stay
N o one there
T o speak to

S o speak to a friend
P et or animal
E ven make a boyfriend
A nd speak to him day and night
K ind and friendly thoughts.

Selina Cox (11)
The Abbey School

Little Speechless Cousin

My aunt just had a baby
He's cute but he can't speak
He can't say yes, no or maybe
If he wants to play hide-and-seek.

If he wants something he just cries
And Aunty has to see what he desires
Like fruit or milk or pies
Or something that he admires.

I wish he could speak like us
And walk and write as well
Without making any fuss
To be honest, I can't tell . . .

Sophie White (11)
The Abbey School

Please Talk Sonnie

My dog called Sonnie
Oh, I do wish he could speak
Even a little word
He would sound so sweet
He is probably scared
But if only he would say something
He tries, but nothing comes out
Oh, I really do wish he could speak
He will never be able to say anything
And never will
He probably feels left out
Nothing to say
I do wish he could speak.

Sophie Armitage (11)
The Abbey School

Away With Words

Today I saw a young boy
He was dressed in black
I didn't think anything was wrong
Until someone tried to speak to him
He could not answer
He just couldn't, he'd lost his voice
It was dark and cold and hollow inside
Just sitting and thinking all day long
Just sitting and waiting for the days to go by
But he realised it was not so bad
He went and learnt sign language
And no one treated him any different
And now he is always happy.

Steven Sparks (11)
The Abbey School

Put In A Box (Labelled A Teenage Thug)

If you could see me you would look away,
If you were near me you would cross the street,
If you could hear me, you would try not to listen,
You would try to ignore me,
You would believe I didn't exist
And you wouldn't waste your time on me.

But why, why do you judge me and stereotype me?
You judge me on others you see, but not on who I really am,
You put me in a box and label me a 'teenage thug'.

You don't like the way I look, you don't like the way I dress,
You think I'm here to impress, I am here to be me
But because you don't know me, you judge me as all the others you see.

But why, why do you judge me and stereotype me?
You judge me on others you see, but not on who I really am,
You put me in a box and label me a 'teenage thug'.

All the times you have seen me, you have always judged me
You feel you have to hate me and that I am only here to make trouble
Well, time's ticking and I'm still here
You don't like me, but why should I care?
You haven't taken the time to know me
So you instantly judge me, because you don't know me.

But why, why do you judge me and stereotype me?
You judge me on others you see, but not on who I really am
You put me in a box and label me a 'teenage thug'.

I am not a teenage thug, I am me.

Kiane Thomas (15)
The Channel School

Don't Do It Mummy

I heard Mum and Dad shouting
It was really, really frightening
I couldn't do anything to block the sound
I heard them say keep her or don't
I had no idea what they were arguing about
Till I realised it was about me.

I really wish I could be free
And swim so far out to sea
So that they wouldn't kill me
I'm so sad because I'm so alone
I hope that Mummy keeps me
After all I'm only a baby
Longing to be free.

As I lay awake and listen to the arguing
I just hope that Mummy wins the fight
So I can wake up every morning
Seeing the world so happy and full of light.

As I woke the next morning, I had such a fright
I heard lots of screaming from my mummy
All I heard her saying was, 'Please don't let it hurt her,'
And all I kept saying was, 'This is the day I die.'
I felt them pull me out and I said,
'Mummy I forgive you,' that's no word of a lie.

So as I land in Heaven upon loads of feathers
I keep thinking, *I wish that Mummy had won the fight.*

Kellie-Louise Bell (15)
The Channel School

Leaving Me, Now And Forever

If I could turn back time
I'd tell you every day that I love you
And I wanted it this way
If I knew we didn't have long
As you were going to a better place
As they say, I'd hold your hand
And try to understand the
Agony and pain.

Seconds turned into minutes
And away you drifted
Minutes turned into hours
Your feelings you would no longer say
Hours turned into days
Quieter and further
Days to weeks, weeks to months
Months to years
Finally you went.

Nothing has changed
I still feel your touch, I still hear your voice
I see you there every night in my dreams
Wishing you were still here by my side
Holding my hand saying
'I love you.'

C Leithead (15)
The Channel School

Old Person

Once there was a man who never stopped to think
That his life was nearly over
But when his life came to an end
He said, 'Is this the end for all, or is it me?
I cannot see because the sky has claws
All that I can see is people walking round and round
I can't even hear a bulldozer being dropped on the ground.
I live in a cellar or that's what it feels like
I sit in my chair every day and night.'

Kieron Knights (14)
The Channel School

My Friend Ellie?

When I was a little girl, I used to sit among the long grass
in the back garden
My mum and dad always used to fight, but I blocked out the noise
and played with Ellie.
Ellie was my best friend, but Mum and Dad could never see her,
She always used to run away, but I always found her
She did a lot of naughty things after my mum or dad shouted at me.
Like the time she cut Mum's hair off, but she never stayed
for the punishment.
Ellie's body soon left, but her thoughts and words still remain.
She told me a man was coming, he was a gonna take Ellie away.
I couldn't let him take my best friend away, but when he came
it was like he had a key
He wound me up so much, I lashed out.
Ellie told me to hit him, again and again
My arms started to ache, I looked at him and went to my room.
Ellie said I had been naughty, I said I wouldn't have dinner.
She said I couldn't have breakfast or lunch the next day either.
I was so weak, and when it came to dinner I couldn't eat,
I had no strength, I collapsed.
My mum took me upstairs to rest. Ellie said this was for the best.
The light went dim but then I started hearing voices.
I didn't hear Ellie, I didn't recognise them.
I opened my eyes to find I was in hospital
My mum explained I had been in a coma for three years
I had jumped out of my window, onto my head
The doctor's found I had schizophrenia and I was being treated
Since then Ellie has never came back, I never got to say goodbye
But I know it's for the best!

Chanelle Penfold (14)
The Channel School

My Time Has Come

Here I am, just lying here, useless
All I hear is voices, speaking in different tongues
The door closes then opens again
The voices are back telling me
What to do.

I try and open my mouth to speak
But I am so weak
I hear Mum's voice
She's crying again
I want to tell her it's all right.

I hear the beeping of the life support
My breath is slowing down
I love you Mum and you Dad
I just want to be happy again
Just like the old times
Let me go Mum
My time has now come.

Lucy Andrews (14)
The Channel School

Feeling Alone

I'm lying here helplessly all alone
No one wants to talk to me
No one wants to tell me why I'm here
But then as I think back - things become more clear.

It feels like I'm in total darkness
Not being able to speak or move
I'm almost totally hopeless
The only thing keeping me alive is hearing people speak.

I think back in my life
Thinking of all the time I've wasted.

If I could turn back time
I would live life to the full
Not spending time wasting my life away.

All I can do now is sit back and hope
That there is someone out there who wants to help.

I keep hearing people saying is she still here
Or is she dead?
I just want to jump up and scream, 'I'm not dead!'

Ashleigh Thomason (14)
The Channel School

Strange Way

People stare at me like I'm a stranger
They look at me in a weird way
They make me feel like I am floating away
I float into the sky
Far, far away
I would love it if I could come back another day.
I will change my life
And say what I say.

Paul Williams (14)
The Channel School

Look Into Your Heart

Look into your heart when I'm not there
And you'll see me
Sat beside you
I'll be your pick-up
When you fall down
I'll be your sunshine
When clouds linger
When rain falls
I'll be there forever
No matter what
My arms will surround you
With love and attention
When people tell you lies
My heart will be your truth
When I look into your eyes
And you look into mine
You will see my passion for you
My hands will massage you
After a hard day
When you can't sleep
I will cloak you in love
And sweep you off your feet
But the best thing I can do
Is to tell you
I love you.

Kyle Ellis (14)
The Channel School

Catwalk

She looks through beautiful green-blue eyes,
Lips all red and plump, shimmering in the dim-lit light,
Hair, all golden and long, gently brushing against her back
                                    on her slim-figured body,
Skin all tanned with a sparkling glow,
All she can see is the world that stands before her.

The adrenaline steadily pumping all round her body,
Faster and faster with the music,
She's just waiting . . .
Waiting to be next,
Next!
The music stops and picks up again with a funky new beat.

She stands there . . .
Stands there all dressed in her high-fashion clothing,
All elegant and flowing, she's hurried onto the runway,
She's just strutting . . .
Strutting with a steady pace,
She hears the crowd begin to mumble and look up at her!

The beauty that walks before them,
Her head held high and her back dead straight,
People's jaws dropping at the sophisticated elegance
                                    she brings to the show,
Could life get any better?

The whole area is black with a mysterious glow,
The runway shines bright white,
The atmosphere so intense it could be cut with a knife,
Spectators' pens clicking and phones going,
                                    looking for the next 'top model'.

She's drawing closer to the end, photographers getting ready,
She poses . . .
She poses with a strong striking look upon her face and body.

Cameras flashing frantically, the room is lit up with electric-blue,
The flashes that stand before her are outstanding,
People begin to clap and cheer!
She doesn't show any nerves but simply smirks, turns
                                    and swiftly struts back.

She passes other young chiselled-like models on her way,
Make-up artists and fashion designers going wild for this new model
behind closed doors,
Frantically running around for the next show, she's finally started
to follow her dream,
Now becoming successful in her life.

Finally . . .
Finally being able to achieve the aspects in life she desires
and has longed for,

On the catwalk . . .
Yes, on the catwalk.

Emma Piper (15)
The Channel School

Paralysed Life

It's a strange place,
I don't know where I am;
I watch people walking through my bed
I see them talking about me;
But I can say nothing to them
I can just talk to myself,
Saying that what a sad life I've got.

People stare at me in sympathy,
I stare at them unconsciously;
Their sympathy doesn't mean anything to me,
The only thing that matters to me is to get up and see the outside world
People in the outside world, might have got a wonderful life,
But look at me, even Hell would be better than my life!

Bibek Koirala (14)
The Channel School

Through The Eyes Of A Cat

I'm about to pounce on my victim
'Stupid little mousy,' I say to myself
I sneak up with a flat crouched back
Wait for three seconds and pounce
1 . . . 2 . . . 3 *pounce*! Darn it, I missed
No mouse for breakfast
I'll just have that yucky Whiskas
Unless it's Felix mmmm
Wait, what's this in my paw, it's a mouse
Mmm that means . . . Felix, I'd better give this present to my owner.

I'm at home now but there is nothing, not even a mouse in the house
I look upstairs for my owner but she isn't there
Outside a lorry is about to pull away with my favourite toy squiggle
I run up and squash myself in a box
Then the door's slammed shut.

I have slept for two hours and I hear a scream
I rush out to find my owner screaming about me, she thinks
                                        I am at home
I sneak up behind her and miaow very loudly, she screams
                                        and jumps with joy.

I'm about to pounce on my prey, I grab it in my paw
'Felix,' my owner calls out to me, I run to the kitchen and miaow with joy
Here on the table is Felix, I drop the mouse by my owner's feet
And enjoy my delicious food.

Allison Dawson (12)
The Channel School

Friends

'All the friends I've ever met,
You're the one I won't forget,
And if I die before you do,
I'll go to Heaven and wait for you,'
And I just have to say,
I love your eyes,
I love your smile,
And it took me a while to find you.

I love your hugs,
I love your kiss,
And they're the things
I'll always miss.

Coral Barnett (15)
The Channel School

Through The Eyes Of A China Doll

I sit up on the top shelf,
I just sit there, looking out
Then there are some loud noises
Like children running about.

A Victorian girl enters the room
Gets me from the shelf
Takes off my hat and brushes my hair
They clearly have got wealth.

The maid comes and opens the curtains
To let the sunlight in
I'm glad to see some sunlight
As it's normally very dim.

But all I am is china
A pretty, but solid face
Quite a basic life really
Standing on a base.

Tarnya Gowar (12)
The Channel School

Trying To Save Lucy

Lucy my cat
Sleeps on the mat.

She died in the road
And got run over by a load.

I loved her, I did
I miss her a bit.

Cute she was
Her heart was the cause.

I would have helped her
But it was late she got run over.

Want her back I do
But I have dogs too.

Ben Millen (12)
The Channel School

The Chair

Sitting in the classroom all day long
Kids come and sit on me as the day goes on.
Oh, does it ache when they swing on me
It's all right I guess, at least I have some company
My friend the table and my friend sitting next to me
It would be better if I had a cushion on this hard old chair
Oh, does it ache when they sit on me
Finally as the school bell goes
I get a rest as the next day grows.

Amy Brown & Drew Phillips (12)
The Channel School

Turn Back Time

If only I could turn back time
Find out the real meaning of life
Watching the clocks ticking as time passes by
Tick-tock, slowly the clock hands move
The world is not going any faster or any quicker
I'm bored, sitting in English
Don't know what to write
I am so confused
My head is spinning.

Stephanie Bridges (15)
The Channel School

Dead In The Tomb

There he stands with a gun
In a tomb deep in the ground
Staring into the dark
With a shiver going up his spine
Scared, not sure what to do
He wants to shoot but he can't
Someone comes, he speaks
Then a bang!
He's there with a gun
In a hand and a dead body on the floor
With blood as red as a rose
Blood pouring from his head like a waterfall
Panicking, not knowing what is happening
Police come pouring out like water
He falls to the floor, laying there
There lies the lady that he has killed
With a blood pond round her head.

Samantha Wilson, Natasha Moon & Kira Cross (15)
The Channel School

Backwards

I've got this time machine just for me,
I can do anything, mess up history,
Like put Henry VIII in a velvet dress,
What would I do next, can you guess?

Shakespeare doing a Beyoncé dance,
Hypnotise David Blaine into a trance,
Elvis can only sing karaoke,
This is fun, *hee, hee, hee!*

Elizabeth I doing break dancing,
Florence Nightingale doing rap singing,
Christopher Columbus dancing at a disco,
What can I do now? I know . . .

Van Gogh doing yoga relaxation lessons,
Picasso releasing his confessions,
Benjamin Franklin working in a chocolate factory, yummyyyy
In my tummyyyyyyyyyyyyyyyy!

George Washington watching his favourite DVD,
King John watching 'EastEnders' on TV,
The Romans in their sports car,
Or at a famous bar.

The Saxons listening to their stereo,
The Vikings singing along to the radio,
Thomas Edison wearing a biker jacket,
Yeah, I've hacked it.

Marilyn Monroe buying a motorbike,
Buddy Holly buying trainers that are Nike,
Marie Curie on her computer,
The Tudors having a race on their scooters.

I've got this time machine just for me,
I can do anything, mess up history.

Natalie Patience & Maddison Shaw (12)
The Channel School

Hurting Love?

Early in the night I lay silently awake
My eyes weeping with the pain
With tears trickling down my face
Why can you not be mine?
Time comes and goes by
With selfishness and greedy eyes
Is this love? Why does it hurt?
Moving on, time goes on!

Amy Sainsbury (15)
The Channel School

Dads

You may like your dad
Or you make think he's bad
But whatever you do
He'll always be there for you.

He'll love you forever and ever
And stop loving you never
His princess you might be
But no more than my dad and me.

Every girl must love their dad
Even if they think he's mad
And whatever he may do
You'll be there for him too.

Dads are great
They could even be your best mate
If you just give them a chance
For their daughters they'll swim to France.

My dad loves me
The best dad in the world, he must be
And whatever you or your dad might do
Remember, he'll always love you.

Cerys Jones (12)
The Channel School

The Siren

The siren went off
Everyone rushed to the shelter
Sitting in a cold and damp area
Listening to the planes
And the bombings
Children crying
The siren sounds 'all-clear'
We walk out into the dust and dirt
And see what is left.

Megan Finnis (13)
The Channel School

Lonely And Blind

Brilliant Buddy is my guide dog
I only have four senses as I lost my eyesight
Tragically five years ago I had an accident
I can feel people staring at me, I don't understand why
I am still human, I just can't see out of my eyes.
At Christmas I can hear the laughter
But I cannot see the smiles
Buddy is my life
Without him I'd be nowhere
I hear the whispers, I feel the pain
I touch to find my way
If only I could see
I could be me.
Buddy is my only friend
I wish I had more
I feel ashamed and lonely
2I'll never have a life, no children and no wedding
Nobody loves me so I hide under my bedding
Buddy sleeps soundly next to me
He is my only company
Tomorrow will be the same as always
The stares, the pain, the loneliness
One day I might be lucky
But until then I will be a lonely blind person
Who no one cares about with a broken heart
And one friend
That's brilliant Buddy.

Naomi Low (12)
The Channel School

Life

Why do we live?
Is our life set out
Or do we chase our own path of life?
Is our life one big game?
But we all know it's going to end.

Aaron Ditcher (12)
The Channel School

Here I Am

Here I am on the street,
Wandering with my aching feet,
Looking out of these tiresome eyes,
As all these years went flying by.

Here I am sitting in the drain,
Surrounded by puddles from pouring rain.
All these thoughts going through my head,
How can Mum kick me out my own bed?

Here I am knocking on the door,
Asking Mum what she did it for?
'As you grew up people ended up dead
I couldn't put up with this,' she said.

The things I did were really bad,
I made everyone really sad.
Running round the neighbourhood, acting a fool,
I wished these stories really weren't true.

All these weapons and a big sharp knife,
I stopped people from having a life.
I'm so sorry Mum, I didn't know what to do,
I hope you believe me and ask Dad for forgiveness too!

Naomi Haigger (15)
The Channel School

Kittens

Oh no, they're back
I've got nowhere to hide
I've got no friends 'cause of the way I look
I can't do anything 'cause no one can understand me
I don't like it, they're always hurting me
I don't like that I can't go out
Wait, that isn't them, it's someone else
He says, 'Come on, I'm getting you out of here.'
Great, now I've to spend time in this cage
Waiting for someone to tell me that I can go home to a new family
That will treat me better than my last family
I'm so happy now I'm in a new family
I'm glad I'm here, they treat me better than my last family.

Kirsty Wire (14)
The Channel School

All By Myself

Why are all these people staring at me?
I'm exactly the same as them
So what if I'm living on my own
They haven't got a right to moan.

I'm surviving by myself
I'm coping all alone
I live in an alleyway
And I'm not going back home.

I'm 14-years old
I'm living on scraps of food
People start throwing abuse at me,
Hey, don't be so rude.

Trying to get to sleep
But all I hear are those storms
Wow! I've found some money
And it's already nearly dawn.

Natasha Robson (14)
The Channel School

A Special Friend Gone!

She was my best friend
She left me here on my own
I'll never forget her, I always think of her
What would it be like if she was still here?
Did she leave because of me?
What did I do? Why did she go?

She was my best friend
We were inseparable, friends forever we always said
We were going to go to college together
We were going to succeed
But she left and I failed.

Now she's gone I don't know who I am
No one cares or understands
Who can I tell? What can I say?
On my own now,
Nothing, no one.

Now I'm on my own I have nothing
But a mate, not even she understands
Gradually picking myself up, smiling
Being happy, then someone mucks it up
Saying her name or killing something of hers.

She came down the other day
Didn't even come and see me
Maybe she doesn't remember me
Forgotten me already
True friends, no friends now she's gone.

She was the other half of me
Completed me, but now she's gone
Now it's just my half
And it's fading, fading quickly.

Amy Rickett (14)
The Channel School

The Dummy

In that forgotten part of town
Where wasted hopes and dreams abound
A wrinkled man with life near its end
In hopes to have at least one friend
Fashioned bits of wood and things
And made a dummy run by strings.

He sat alone for hours on end
Conversing with his only friend
And found delight within the fact
That he controlled its every act
He told it how he never had
A chance, since all his luck was bad
Although he'd tried so to succeed -
The dummy nodded and agreed.

And how his journeys in romance
Had never given him a chance
And wasn't it a crying shame
That he was always held to blame
When everyone knew, oh so well
That life is but a living Hell
Controlled by lust and power and greed?
The dummy nodded and agreed.

With patience that would rival saints
That dummy sat through all complaints
And, with each little expert tug
He'd droop his head or bow or shrug
And give some comfort to the man
Who held his lifelines in his hand
And helped to fill a lonely need
When he just nodded and agreed.

Senility increased with time
As did the old man's pantomime
And feverish fingers pulled with glee
The dummy's dance of misery.

They never left each other's side
Until the day both stopped and died
We found them lying, hand in hand
The dummy - and his wooden friend.

Amy Neale (14)
The Channel School

Abandoned Animal

My owner doesn't love me
I was left under a tree.

I was in a cardboard box
And I heard a fox.

It turned dark, I think it was night
Something was shining at me, it was a light.

In the distance I could hear an owl
I suddenly headr a little miaow.

I tried to escape
But I fell in a lake.

I struggled to swim to the edge
I rolled into a hedge.

Hands picked me up
I thought *I'm in luck*.

They gave me a big cuddle
My head was in a muddle.

They took me home
I heard a friendly tone.

Karianne Jewkes (13)
The Channel School

I Love You

I love him so much,
So much I don't even know
He's always in my head
No matter where I go.
In my head I'm in a pretty pink dress
As he always treats me like a princess!
If I lost him
I would be sad, lonely and dim
I wouldn't know what to do
I would just want to say, I love you!

Lucy Davis (14)
The Channel School

Wedding Bells

Ding-dong, the bells have gone
Ding-dong, the clock's struck one
That could only mean one thing
The force of these magical rings.

The vows that we share
Show that we care
The meaning of love
Flies like white doves.

The church choir sing
While we exchange our rings
The streams of confetti
Look like spaghetti.

Now it's the end of June
Off we go to our honeymoon
Now we're back, nice and brown
We're glad we're back in our hometown.

Naomi Dewberry (12)
The Channel School

I'm Being Bullied

Bullying is bad
Bullying is wrong
It happens to me all day long
I am a victim, yes it's true
I don't know the bully
Is it you?

The text messages keep coming
When I come home from school
When I read them
They say I'm a fool.

I ask myself, why, why is it me?
I sit here crying
Whilst they laugh with glee.

When I stand up
They push me back down
They look, they stare
And then they frown.

I take a knife from the kitchen drawer
The tears are coming and fall on the floor
In the end I split my wrist
Now I'm invisible
Just like I wished.

Sophie Phillips (12)
The Channel School

Untitled

I look outside and see
Joy
Happiness
And ecstasy
Then I know right next door
A man who can hurt
A man that can kill
A hear a knock at the door
Is it him? Oh no
I've got to hide
I can't
Stuck in here, no one can help
I am old, fragile
And helpless.

He has a key, he's opening the door
No one knows
No one can help
The door is creaking
Is he in?
I try to get up
I can't
I take a look outside again
I see one last time the
Joy
Happiness and
Ecstasy
He's here
He's calling
Then . . .

Mark Harman (14)
The Channel School

Untitled

I wanted it to be like it used to be
When it was just you and me
We had fun all the time
That was when you were really kind.

Then it all changed a lot
That was when my little sister came along
In the night it was wa-wa-wa
It used to be ha-ha-ha
Then it changed a lot.

When she came along I changed
I was really naughty
My mum used to call me a pain
That was when it all changed.

My mum got rid of my dad
Then I was really sad
But I still saw him
And in my dreams.

Jessica Bunker (12)
The Channel School

Alone In The Dark

I'm lying in the dark
Not knowing what will come
Crawling in fear
And I shed a tear.

I close my eyes
And dream of happiness
Woken up with another bruise
And now I know what's coming.

I pray to God
That Mum won't shout at me
Or even worse
Mum's boyfriend won't hit me.

I crawl up in a corner
Thinking about Mum
I know that inside
She really does love.

I go to school
And get bullied there
I come back home
And get chucked around there.

I go to my secret place
And there's no one there
No one to hurt me
And I'm not afraid to stare.

Chereece Horton (14)
The Channel School

Individuality

What's the point of living?
No one gives a s***
We're all the same
Nothing to gain
And my mind's full of rage . . .

What's the point of living?
As I sit on this damp and bleak road on my own
With the lives of other's shown
I hardly have time to think of my own.

How can we evolve, if we don't like change?
I can see my destiny just in range
But I can't pursue it because everyone's scared of change.

I se the secrets of others, revealed when I lay back
It makes me feel awful, just like people giving me flack.

James Richards (14)
The Channel School

Dream On!

If I could turn back time
Not a lot would change
Maybe just a few things
I want to make people happy
Not the fear they have now.

I wouldn't let people suffer
As all they want is a normal life
Like everyone else
As all they want is to be happy.

I would build a machine
That could blow away
All the evil people
That came our way.

I would blow away
All the pain people feel
Physically and mentally
It's not fair, no one deserves it.

But maybe I should get real
I could never turn back time
It's not reality, it's just a dream
I can't do that, not me
I'm just an ordinary 14-year-old
Whose life is, just a dream.

Laura McMurray (14)
The Channel School

Lonely

It all went wrong
Because of that moron
He took me for a fool
Which I suppose I am, the tool.

I know that I should love her
But I find it really hard
I can't even touch her
I find it too hard.

He left me when I told him
Pregnant with his kid
He told me that I was a rat
And I never saw him again.

My mum was disappointed
That I could be so stupid
She kicked me out
Her and that lout
Never seen them since.

Now I'm on my own
All alone
Just me
Me and a screaming baby.

Debbi-Louise Cole (14)
The Channel School

No Home

I used to have it all, a family, a home,
But now I've lost it all, no family, no home.
A happy family goes by and I ask myself, 'Why?
Why did I end up with nowhere to go?'

It seems simple to look at why I ran away
The endless waterfall of arguments
The beatings that came my way
So I took some cash and searched for a new life
Now I look at it, I feel full of strife.

I spent my last pound on a small piece of food
Now I feel hungry and don't know what to do
Should I turn back to a family and a home
Or should I continue on, no family no home?

Kyle Fairlie (14)
The Channel School

All The Time In The World

I used to think I had time
All the time in the world
I used to think . . .

But now that I have no time
I ask myself, *What have I done?*
What have I done?

I look outside my window and see people
People think they have time
All the time in the world.

And here I am at the end
At the end of my days, knowing that one day
These people will realise that they don't have time
That they don't have all the time in the world.

Nobody has all the time in the world.

Josie Frost (16)
The Channel School

Different

I see you strutting towards me,
Wearing your Reebok hoody
You slowly walk like you have a bad leg
Yet you think you're 'gangsta'.

You think you're tough
Because you smoke underage
It's your lungs slowly blocking up
You shout abuse at me
Sometimes throw objects at me
And kick puddles at me
Just because I have a wheelchair
And I look different this doesn't mean
I'm a different species.

I'm now in my room with the door locked
Sitting on my bed
I think my life isn't worth it
I take this blade slowly
Cut my skin, I see blood which slowly trickles out.

I lie back and shut my eyes
Now everyone is in black
My family are crying
They wish they had helped me
But it's too late, I'm dead
I'm now playing poker with the Grim Reaper.

Lee Collin (15)
The Channel School

If You Could

Why do we live?
Who decides?
Why do we die?
Who decides?

If you could, would you?

Is there a Heaven?
Is there a Hell?
Is there a God?
Is there a Devil?

If you could, would you?

Who am I?
Where am I?
Who are you?
Where are you?

If you could, would you?

No one knows.

Charllotte Kiddell (15)
The Channel School

Homeless Teen

Soz 4 wot I hav done
Pleaz don't h8 me
Pleaz don't find me
4 I'm in a betta place
Send . . .

And I'm off down the road to nowhere
Nowhere to run
Nowhere to hide
Nowhere to stay
I'm homeless.

I wish I could turn back time
Change things
And maybe
Just maybe
I wouldn't be homeless.

Good times and bad times will stick in my mind
My friends
My family
They don't mean anything anymore.

As I sit here on the street
Begging
'Please Sir. Please Sir, have you got any change?'

Amy Sawyer (16)
The Channel School

Life

When I was three
My closest friend was a boy
He lived on the farm next to me
His name was Roy!

When I was nine
We were inseparable
We went to the same school
He was so loveable.

When I was fourteen
We started dating
It was a bit strange at first
But then it was amazing!

When I was nineteen
He proposed and I said yes
We planned the wedding
But it was quite a mess!

When I was twenty-four
I was married and had a baby
My life seemed at its peak
It couldn't get any better!

When I was forty
The love of my life fell ill
He had cancer
He didn't have long to live

Now I'm ninety
He died forty years ago
Life just hasn't been the same since then
He made it ten years!

If I could turn back time I would
I'd make it me that was ill
I'd give him more time
If only he would come back.

Now this is my last few hours
This is my life from the beginning.

Lynne Mockridge (15)
The Channel School

The Day My Life Ended

The day I saw
A window was open
A light was shining through
In the distance a figure, tall and bold
He stared in the distance
Me, why me?

I wondered what was happening
My eyes were like a river
On a mountain running down
Get me.

I sat there watching a thing go *beep, beep beep*
Then in stepped a figure in the distance
Went quiet and still.

The final day I said goodbye
I cried a little
My heart was like a thunderstorm crashing inside me
A box lying there, fire surrounding
Then the doors shut, closed
One memory
One Mum.

Monique Phillips (15)
The Channel School

Coma

Life is such a bitch
Ten days ago I was left to die in a ditch
Now my life is covered in darkness
I miss my life
With my wife and kids.

This coma is a new step of life
My family are affected
But look at it through my eye
I've had it.

I am lying in my bed
People talk to me like I am dead
I can *hear you*
I scream
I can smell food
Please feed me, I am so hungry.

I can't wait until I get up
I want to walk, but I can't be bothered now
I want to feel the wind on my face
And the kiss of my wife.

There is nothing left for me
To look forward to now.

Barney Stephens (15)
The Channel School

All I Ever Did Was Love You

All I ever did was love you
You took everything away from me
You stole my heart
You stole my dreams
I thought I'd never be alone.

The way you used to look at me
The way you used to smile
Things will never be the same without you
You can't always see the pain someone feels
I'm crying inside, no one knows it but me.

You hurt me so bad, you don't know how much it hurts
Not being close to you
All I ever did was love you
Now it's time for someone to love me back.

Love is like being in your own world
Once you're there it's hard to go back
My dream was to have everlasting love
And my wish was for it to be with you
All I ever did was love you.

Christina Parker (15)
The Channel School

Ghetto

What do you know about the struggles that my people went through
So you can live the way you do now?
What do you know about people dying before their time
So you can eat the food you do now?
What do you know about escaping from that prison camp
To see how you are now?

I'm not sitting here wondering
What you know about Gorder Island
Where all us slaves were shipped from
What do you know about . . .
Being born in America to avoid immigration?

How the hell did I deserve to be placed in this situation
With nobody's concern?
I'll fry your head, like a project perm
Bullets burn, my right hand's in an urn
I play my part, well respected . . .
Every minute . . .
Every second.

Streets I call home, there's no one to call on
Every man for himself, I come from the bottom
I've been behind the trigger
I've been in front of the bullet, but where I'm from
We don't think about it, we pull it
Coz these teens killing teens for half of their jeans.

Anthony Wire (15)
The Channel School

Me?

The searing sun blazed with its usual brilliance,
As I bathed in its warmth,
    But yet the heat does not reach me.

Ignorant children laughed and screamed in merriment,
Seemingly to be without a care in the world,
    Ignorant of the darkness tainting their innocence.

Birds sang sweetly and joyfully,
As they sat from a tree in full blossom,
    But I do not hear the notes of this spectacular piece.

A soothing breeze caresses me gently,
Bringing along the refreshing aroma of summer,
    But I lay on the slightly damp grass, unaffected by it all.

This is the masterpiece God has created
And I am the stain which blemishes it.
I am that smudge, that taint, that poison,
Which plant its root to spread and infect.
I do not belong.

I lived with this knowledge since the age of three,
The burden of this undeniable truth grew heavier as the years went by.

The existence of the mother I have never met was wiped out,
replaced with the unwanted arrival of my presence.
    Loneliness reared its ugly head and sniffed.

My abusive father threw biting words at me daily,
Accompanied by many encounters with the 'Whip'
    Loneliness noticed me for the first time.

The children and teacher alike avoided me,
Unnerved by the harsh reality of my everyday life.
    Loneliness eyed me hungrily as saliva dripped from its gaping jaw.

    Deserted by all who never batted an eye at me,
    Expelled by a school which never accepted me,
    Kicked out of a house which neglected me.

I looked at loneliness in the eye, as its lips curved slowly in
a malicious grin.
   The moment has arrived
   My fate was decided
As loneliness forever embraced me in its dark, freezing and unrelenting
grasp.

Nga-Kam Mou (15)
The Channel School

Recurring Dream

I keep dreaming that I'm falling
There's no safety net
You look right up and see me broken
I keep hoping that the whispers fade away
My past disasters leave me in chains
I drop the shackles but still . . .

I'm walking a tightrope
Between who I love and what I know
I'm watching the sharks lick their lips
As they circle far below.

I keep dreaming that I'm falling
There's no safety net.

Luke Anderson (15)
The Channel School

The Celtic Gladiator

The innards sprayed upon my face symbolised all the death
I dropped the head laden with filth
And ripped the blunt sword from his chest
'Hail Caesar,' I yelled as he lowered the down-faced thumb
He grinned the grin of death
'Release Claudius, kill the bloody Celt.'
A tear rolled down my face
But I knew it would come forth
The gate raised to show the face of a creature
So bold and angry he seemed
He spun the fork and raised the shield
The spearhead I tore from my leg
I started running, ran and ran
Till I could run no more
For the fork lodged inside my chest broke my run
I started pulling forward, forward and forward yet more.
'Thank you,'
I uttered, I thrust the sword into his throat
His blood spraying on my face
Shocked cries rang in my ears
I fell upon the bloody, sandy floor
The sand reminded me of the shores of England
Where me and my daughter played on weekends
The tears started running onto the floor
I started weeping.
Wept and wept
Till I could weep no more.

Alex Terry (12)
The Channel School

What People Think

People see me as a criminal
Nicking food from shops
People see me as a murderer
Seeking people in revenge
People see me as a rapist
Hunting people for my benefit
People see me as suicidal
Killing myself because of what I had done
People see me as beating my family
Taking it out on other people.

But all I am is a person
In prison for drinking and driving.
But people don't know
That I had to get to my dad's funeral
Now I wish I was dreaming
And that funeral was mine.

Hannah-Lee Capon (12)
The Channel School

Who? You!

I am the deaf, the mute, the blind
In their eyes I would be,
I am the lame, the cripple, the freak
I might as well be,
I am the violent, the destruction, the evil
How could I ever be?
I am the love, the kind, the sweetness
As if they would believe me.
I am the shrewd, the coward, the lonely
In their eyes they make me,
I have given up on life. Final!
And it's all their eyes that force me . . .

But should I let them get to me?
I will be the strength, the mentality, the might!
They pile their slander onto me,
I shake it off, the shield, the wall, the fortress!
I won't let the lies penetrate me,
You look at me, the gaze, the glare, the stare!
But they don't get to me,
You're puzzled, outraged, infuriated!
Your words and looks won't get to me,
I stand steady, calm, waiting . . .
You don't get me!

Jordan Latore (16)
The Channel School

Away With Words

Crunch, crunch, crunch,
Rubbish, trees swaying
Clouds are coming, *crash!*
It starts to rain, oh no lightning.

Windows creaking with the doors
Gaps in the window whistling
Then the leaves start to crunch
Twigs fall off the trees.

Then it goes quiet
People clean up
Then it looks calm
And then there is a big *crash.*

It all starts again,
Bins flying around
Plant pots fly
Will it ever stop?

Jack Milner (11)
The Thomas Aveling School

A Windy Day

Fresh breeze blowing
Dark, dusty night
Brown trees swaying
Very stormy night.

The door creaks open
When the wind pushes it open
Leaves being swept off the floor
And the crunch of the leaves.

The leaves are flying off the floor
The leaves cover the people
And the whistling of the wind
When the trees sway.

Every night it gets dark
And then the people
Run around because of
The whistling of the wind.

Connor Starkey (11)
The Thomas Aveling School

Windy Day

Crispy leaves blowing
Spooky trees swaying
Gloomy clouds gathering
Raging winds whistling.

Whistling winds raging
Cold destructive breeze
Twisting and turning, gusty winds
Howling through the towns.

Howling, howling, leaving nothing
But dust
All that is left is a dry creaky town
The town is awfully cold and bare.

Cold and bare the town is left
The terrible raging wind has gone
All that's there is a gust pushing dust
Creaky doors, dry leaves and a cold breeze.

Cherylann Howland
The Thomas Aveling School

Away With Words

Crunch, crunch, crunch, owww
As the wind is howling
The freezing cold air
Knocking leaves off trees.

On the floor the leaves lay
Swaying everywhere
The dusty air
Makes us all cough.

The freezing cold air
Makes us cold
We wrap up
But we are still cold.

Scary, howling air
Pushing everything in sight
Then it dies down
Till it's no more.

Jessica Potter (11)
The Thomas Aveling School

Windy Day

Swish, swish, swish,
I can feel the wind blowing
Right through my hands
I can't believe it's making my hair stand.

What's that whistle?
I can hear it as faint as a thistle
That I think is the leaves
Swaying in the breeze.

The wind is creating destruction
Crunching all the leaves
Destroying buildings
And collapsing all trees!

Now as the wind disappears
Destroying its last object
The only word I can say is,
'Goodbye!'

Rahul Attra
The Thomas Aveling School

Windy Day

The trees are swaying
The leaves are crunching
The clouds are out
The wind is dark and scary.

The howling noise, the green trees
Raging along the dusty road
Making so much noise
The neighbours can't sleep.

The doors are creaking and slamming
The streets are dusty
It looks so gloomy
I feel cold and scary.

The leaves are blowing everywhere
The dust is falling in our eyes
But the breeze is so nice and calm
That makes me comfy in our house.

Farhana Begum (11)
The Thomas Aveling School

Windy Day

Trees blowing side to side
Clouds gathering, starting to rain
Dusty wind up and down
Please, please go away.

Leaves falling from the tree
The sky is falling deeply
Rain, rain I hate you
Please, please go away.

Leaves, leaves rustling past the town
Rain, rain falling across the countryside
Thunder, thunder shooting across the street
Wind, wind blowing past the world.

Rain, rain you're so wet
Wind, wind you're so cold
Thunder, thunder you're so loud
Leaves, leaves you're so creepy.

Jacky Zhu
The Thomas Aveling School

Away With Words

The sunny day is swept away
By the windy way
There is no sun
On that day.

On a windy day
The leaves come
Out to play
On that day.

The wind twirls and swirls
And destroys the day
With its howl
And takes away
All the motorway.

The wind blows
Very hard against the trees
A few fall
Then the sun will set.

Amy Louise Strevens (11)
The Thomas Aveling School

A Windy Day

The wind is a destructive thing
Hats and leaves flying everywhere
Trees swaying in the breeze
Tiles flying off the roof.

But the wind is not all bad
Sometimes even graceful
Not always in a form of a monster
In the breeze.

The wind is like a person
It has two sides
Dark and light, bad and good
A light breeze and gale force winds.

Little kids jumping in the leaves
The leaves crunching
Flying everywhere
In a light breeze.

Joshua Banfield
The Thomas Aveling School

A Windy Day

It's a breezy day
All the trees are going to sway
Swish, swish, swish
Now I want this to stop
I really do wish.

The wind is howling
It seems like a soft growling
The leaves are crispy
And the wind blows wispy.

Wooooooooooo
Listen to that wind flow past my room
Bang, crash, roar
There goes all that rubbish
Please, no more.

Soon the wind dies down
Into a soft cosy breeze
People are smiling
And so are the bees.

Amy Dawe (11)
The Thomas Aveling School

A Windy Day

Breeze in the air
Leaves lie beneath my feet
Tilting tiles fall from the rooftops
Trees shatter greenhouse windows.

People stay at home
Wind rages through my street
Getting closer and closer
It strikes!

The wind hits my house hard
Like a tiger catching its prey
The house shakes with fear
Like an earthquake at its worst.

The rest of the street
Stand and stare
As the wind destroys my house
It suddenly *stops!*

Jack Johnston
The Thomas Aveling School

A Windy Day

Leaves keep blowing
Trees keep swaying
Now I'm going
To go playing.

Dark night comes quick
Now I have butterflies
And I feel sick
Morning comes.

All you see are leaves on the floor
Wind still whistling past my window
Now it's calm I can come out my door
All of a sudden I can hear a roar.

When I come back to my house
Crispy leaves on my drive
All I see is a tiny mouse
Slowly the wind dies down
Just like a noise fading in the distance.

Kieran Oliver (11)
The Thomas Aveling School

Windy Day

Dusty, gusty, blows me away
Whistling along with the trees
Dust blows along roads
The wind disrupting people's sleep.

Rustling, jostling, throwing the leaves
Raging along the deep blue seas
Cats run to their homes
The wind creaking all front doors.

Crispy and sleekly the wind goes
Chucking away all in its path
The wind approaches from the mist
It's awful when people fall sick.

The wind, the wind
So loud and ready to pounce
The wind, the wind, oh what to do
I hope it doesn't come for you.

Matthew Forster (12)
The Thomas Aveling School

A Windy Day

As the wind passes by it sweeps the leaves from the ground
You hear the crispness of the leaves as the wind crushes them until
they are no more.

It terrifies the trees as it rages through the town
It twists and turns until it finds the object it wants to force
And then without anyone knowing it pounds it like a fist
Against a plant and tips the object right over.

As the whistling of the wind calls its dog
It passes through the park, past the lady who feeds the pigeons
Past the old men who play chess, then slowly dies down to a breeze.

As the breeze wisps through the gate it tests the spiders' webs until
they break
It seeps under the door and blows into the room
It pokes at the fire and blows and blows until the flames die out.

Daniel Duncanson (11)
The Thomas Aveling School

Windy Day

The door creaks, squeaks
As it sways
Breeze blowing through the window
Because it's a windy day.

The leaves, munch, crunch
As they fly
Swirling, swinging
It will never die.

The wind howls, scowls
As it twirls
Picking up everything in its way
As it swirls, twirls away.

Wind in the night
Wind in the day
Wind in every direction
It's a windy day.

Sam Simmons (12)
The Thomas Aveling School

Away With Words

Windy winds howl in the night
Wind swooshing through the kites
Leaves blowing in the sky
Leaves bye-bye-bye.

Branches hitting each other
Cuddling each other like lovers
Gates creaking and banging
Tyres hanging from trees - just hanging.

When the winds howl
They sound ever so loud
Trees looking so alive
Buzzing bees going to their beehives.

Sitting there
Looking so scared
People wrapping up in more clothes
Just going to the shops to buy their daily loaves.

Kayleigh Wells (11)
The Thomas Aveling School

Christmas!

My best time of the year is Christmas
I love all of my presents
And in the field opposite my house
My dad admires the pheasants!

I love Christmas presents
I tear them open with glee
And as I unwrap
My parents stare at me!

Yeah!

C hristmas dinner and Christmas cake
H appy faces all around
R eligious people gathering around and celebrating
I cy and snowy weather like a lovely winter wonderland
S parkling lights on houses at night
T ree lights twinkling in people's windows
M erry Christmas
A child getting all excited as they wait for bedtime
S anta coming on Christmas Eve.

Laura Beale (11)
The Thomas Aveling School

If I Turned Back Time To When I Was Born!

If I turned back time
My mum would be so glad saying, 'She's all mine!'
My parents would talk to me,
'Oh how beautiful is she?'

My parents would be so *proud!*
And I was drawing a *big* crowd
I know I am really cute
But I wish I could put all the visitors on mute!

When everyone talked to me
It didn't make sense
I don't talk like that
As I got older I got a bit more fat
Lots of money spent on presents for me
People saying, 'Oh it's a she!'

I was 7lb 3oz when I was born,
'Hello beautiful,' said my papa John
I am the one
That started all of the family
Fun!

Molly Teresa Lane (11)
The Thomas Aveling School

Good Memories

When I was young my nan lived by the sea
Every time I went down, we went there
We had our dinner on the shore, even in the wind
We didn't care
We looked for crabs and jellyfish under rocks
Once the tide had gone in we walked in the mud
And I lost most of my shoes.
All of these good memories are from when she was alive
Nan died two days after my birthday on the 27th June 2000
Thanks Nan, for all the good memories I've got today.

Kieran Clarke (11)
The Thomas Aveling School

Christmas

Christmas is a time for fun
Opening all the presents
You just wish you hadn't begun
Because you know it's going to end in a second.

Christmas is a time for family
To chat to them and give them your love
So come on Emily
Let's go outside and put on our gloves.

Christmas is a time for snow
Come on put on your scarf
Be careful now and aim low
Don't be shy now, it's only for a laugh.

Joe Wilkinson (15)
The Thomas Aveling School

My Sweet Valentine

My love greeted me with flowers
And chocolates on our special day
St Valentine's he took me to dinner and proposed
The ring was beautiful and glistened like the stars in the night sky
He walked me home and came in for coffee
He is handsome with his blond hair and his sparkly blue eyes
like the ocean
My heart aches for my love and I will love him for ever and always.

Danielle Clare Scott (13)
The Thomas Aveling School

Football

Man U, the best from all the rest,
There at the top with no mess.
Cristiano Ronaldo with all the skills,
Keeps coming like the phone bills.
Van Der Sar with the great saves,
Which the superb strikers gave.
Neville tackling with possession,
Making him an injured man.

Chelsea, second of the table,
Not very stable.
Buying Ballack and Shevcenko,
Scoring in one good blow.

Liverpool hunting for first place,
Don't have enough power and pace.
Alonso scoring a wicked goal,
Gerrard having a big role.

Jamee Salam (13)
The Thomas Aveling School

Teachers

Teachers, teachers, teachers
Are mean and nasty creatures
They talk, talk, talk a lot
They make you fall asleep.

They give you a detention
Because you want attention
They give them for the slightest reason
I missed the bus again today.

One day I went to play
With all my friends
One teacher came to say,
'You haven't done any work today.'

They give you hard maths questions too!

Jass Powar
The Thomas Aveling School

Away With Words

I'm going away on a plane
I'm going, I am so scared.

I have no words to describe it,
Will I know the language?

I feel so worried
I feel so scared
But I have to leave my family behind.

Marina Popova
The Thomas Aveling School

The Sad Cow

The sad cow was in the field
Feeling down, lonely and depressed
because she had no friends.

She lay down staring at the grass
Long and lush and free
The dew sparkled like diamonds
She longed to have friends.

Taking in the beauty, it made her more depressed
The farmer came to get her
To put her to rest.

The cow said, 'Please don't kill me
I only want friends.'
The farmer sent her to a ranch
And the cow lived happily ever after with her new friends.

Simon Baldwin
The Thomas Aveling School

My Dad's A Vampire!

It's midnight
And it is dark and gloomy
My windows are open
And my curtains hoist up in the air
My door opens and closes
And I hear my lock go
Something is in my room with me
I can hear my floor go *creak, creak, creak*
And I see a shadow
Of something with a cape
It's coal-black
Then suddenly . . .
'Argh!'
I scream as my lamp turns bright
It's my dad with his dressing gown on
Saying goodnight
He kisses my cheek
And turns out the light
Then leaves my room
Thank goodness it wasn't a vampire
Then a sudden shock came to me
Another shadow I can see
I can hear a creak
If my dad and mum
Aren't in my room
Who is that?
The shadow has gone
'Argh!'

Jade Dowse (12)
The Thomas Aveling School

Homeless

I'm homeless and sad,
Feeling unwanted and bad.
Cold and lonely,
Missing my home.

No one to talk to,
Nowhere to go.
Getting in fights wherever I go,
Where I am, nobody knows.

I wanna go home,
Because I'm all alone.
My mum would be glad,
But Vince thinks I'm bad.

I feel like I'm invisible,
I really want something edible.
I'm homeless and sad,
Feeling unwanted and bad.

Shelby Wheller
The Thomas Aveling School

Homeless

Most of the homeless
Are usually penniless
They haven't got a home
Neither have they go a mobile phone.

The haven't any food
They're always in a mood
They haven't got a drink
They never think.

People treat them bad
It makes them really sad
They get called names
They have never been on an aeroplane.

They never wash
Cos they haven't got any dosh
It's usually men, they have long hair
All their kids get put into care.

Lewis Slaughter (14)
The Thomas Aveling School

Homeless

I've been walking the streets for days
Hurry up the DSS I want my pay
I'm sitting here in the freezing ice
People here are not very nice
When I stop someone to ask them
All they say is, 'Who do you think I am?'

William Connell (14)
The Thomas Aveling School

Homeless

You are walking down the street you always see a tramp
All they can do is sleep
It's always cold and damp
They open their eyes and give you a peep.

The only thing they can do is beg
They're always saying, 'Please can I have some money?'
All you can do is spare an arm and a leg
'Cause they don't eat, all they have is a small tummy.

All you feel is, someone give them a home
They just need to eat
Unfortunately they can't even afford a mobile phone
It would be better than being out in the street.

All they need is a good friend
They just need a lot of care
You're always seeing them from end to end
If only people were nice and fair.

Jay Taylor (13)
The Thomas Aveling School

Life

We begin life very tiny
And as a baby are very whiny
We get spoilt rotten
And are cuddled in cotton!

We then become a toddler
And start to walk
We then begin to express ourselves
And soon enough we talk.

At five we go to school
And like to play the fool
We run around the playground
'Oh look what I've found!'

Years and years go by
And then we go to work
I hope to earn lots of money
And I'll become a clerk!

Charlotte Brincat (12)
The Thomas Aveling School

Life's A Challenge . . .

Challenges always come my way,
I like to complete them, day by day.
Whether they're good or whether they're bad,
When I complete them: I'm always glad.

Challenges big or challenges small,
Whether climbing a mountain or kicking a ball;
Completing an English, maths or French test,
Always trying harder to be the best.

Friendship's a challenge and school too,
But we must stick together through and through.
We mustn't give up or all is lost
And I, for one, don't want to pay that cost.

Life's one big challenge - the hardest of them all,
But when such a task comes round to call,
I open the door and welcome it in
And put all my worries in the bin!

Amy Gray (13)
The Thomas Aveling School

More Than Words

The accident happened, I was not to survive
In the hospital, they hoped me revived
Through the darkness came a light
Something else, something right

I thought about the time I wasted
Through stupid acts like alcohol tasting
Now in a bed with no one here
My thoughts rage past, I cannot steer

The car was a trick, a clever delusion
Now I'm paying my retribution
If I had the chance to go back
Common sense that I would not lack

A chance to avoid that car
A chance to avoid the feelings I'm feeling
More than words.

Sean Kollath-Newport (13)
The Thomas Aveling School

Life Is Life

Life is like a box of chocolates
You don't know what's inside
Life has its ups and downs
It also has its highs and lows

In life anything could happen
You don't know what is around the corner
Life is what you make it

The more you put in
The more you get out
Life is the biggest price of all
So live life to the full.

Chris Bailey (13)
The Thomas Aveling School

What If I Could?

If I could turn,
Turn back in time,
What would I change?
How would I stop poverty,
Or would I stop war?

What do you think I'd see?
A poor beggar,
A homeless child,
A hopeless baby?

What would I wear?
Would I wear a posh frock?
Would I wear a rag?
Would I wear a bathing suit,
Or would I have a fag?

What is the world like?
I take a look,
I see heaps of rubbish,
I see muddy paths,
I see a horrible future,
I see a dirty world.

So here I am,
I see dirty streets,
I see a future,
The future has to change.

Willow Burford (13)
The Thomas Aveling School

Give A Voice To A Person That Can't Speak

Give a voice so someone can speak,
To listen, to understand, for someone to speak,
To explain, to tell, for someone to speak,
So think about all the people who cannot speak,
So be grateful that you have a voice so you can speak.

Georgia McIlheron (11)
The Thomas Aveling School

Homeless

No one to talk to
No family to see
How did I get like this? I'm lonely and sad
If I went home my mum would be so glad.

My bum's gone numb and no one's polite
I don't know how but I get in lots of fights
I'm scared and ignored
And during the day I get so bored.

I would like something to play with
Like some cards or a dice
The people that pass me
Are not very nice.

I feel dirty and smelly
I've got a pain in my belly
I have nowhere to go
When it starts to snow.

Grace Barker (14)
The Thomas Aveling School

The Homeless

We have no home, we have no money,
the situation to us isn't funny.
We never have food,
because of this we're very rude.
The comments we get aren't very nice,
they leave us freezing in the ice.
Our clothes are dirty,
we have mud on our faces
and we lived in some weird places.
Doorways are the place to sleep,
finding the right one is hard to keep.
We get woken up
and have to move along,
until another doorway is free,
until then it's just you and me.

Jessica Ellis-Lineham (13)
The Thomas Aveling School

Away With Words

All the homeless have no homes
They hear all the people's moans
They hardly have any food
They all get in a bad mood.

People treat them very bad
Living that way drives them mad
They smell and don't wash
All the people walk past are posh.

All the people call them names
As they get off their buses and trains
They have long scruffy hair
Some kids go into care.

They never hardly get a drink
If they do it's gone in a blink
All the homeless are mostly men
They get their homes at number 10.

Luke Crookes (14)
The Thomas Aveling School

Homeless

I'm a poor little boy sleeping in the street
I don't like most of the people I meet
I look in the bins for food and drink
I wish I had a toilet and sink.

I'm sitting here freezing like ice
All the passers-by are not very nice
I sit in a doorway all on my own
I think to myself, *I wish I had a home.*

I wander around the streets all day
Loads of people tell me to go away
I get insulted by this behaviour
I hope the DSS will do me a favour.

When I stop someone to ask for money
They laugh at me as if I am funny
It makes me feel like sinking so deep
So I lay in my doorway and go to sleep.

Michael Olsen (13)
The Thomas Aveling School

Homeless

I am a homeless boy
With no food or drink,
Cars go by
As I blink.

I walk around
Looking for space,
The doorways are full,
I check just in case.

I see an old man with grey hair,
He offers me an apple and pear.
I find a bench and sit down to eat,
I feel sick now and look at my feet.

I've no employment,
I need no job,
I'm cold at the moment,
I need a Hobnob.

Billy Cook & Nathan Baker (13)
The Thomas Aveling School

A Poem On Life!

You open your eyes
And when you hear the birds singing
And you think how lucky you are to be alive
Fit and healthy.

Every day is the same
Like when you go to school
You take the same root every day
You know everyone.

But the good thing about this
Is that it might be the same
But you should be thinking
How lucky you are to walk
And do exciting things.

Alex Busher (12)
The Thomas Aveling School

Life

Life can sometimes be unfair and unkind,
It can be hurtful and it plays with your mind,
Life can be happy or sad,
It can make you good or bad.

Life can reward you if you put your mind to it,
Just try your best and you'll get it.
There's always something to look forward to in life,
With the right attitude you'll succeed.

Nathan Bit-David
The Thomas Aveling School

Young Writers Information

We hope you have enjoyed reading this book - and that you will continue to enjoy it in the coming years.

If you like reading and writing poetry drop us a line, or give us a call, and we'll send you a free information pack.

Alternatively if you would like to order further copies of this book or any of our other titles, then please give us a call or log onto our website at www.youngwriters.co.uk

Young Writers Information
Remus House
Coltsfoot Drive
Peterborough
PE2 9JX

(01733) 890066